ALL-TIME FUNNIEST JOKES

ABOUT HOLIDAYS

Little Mitchie
an imprint of Mitchell Lane

Creating Young Nonfiction Readers

Little Mitchie lets children delve into nonfiction at young reading levels. Young readers are introduced to new concepts, facts, ideas, and vocabulary.

Tips for Reading Nonfiction with Young Readers

Talk about Nonfiction

Begin by explaining that nonfiction books give us information that is true. The book will be organized around a specific topic or idea, and we may learn new facts through reading.

Look at the Parts

Most nonfiction books have helpful features. Our *Little Mitchie* titles include color photographs and graphic aids, a table of contents, a glossary, and an index. Share the purpose of these features with your reader.

Color Photos and Graphic Aids

A lot of information can be found by "reading" photos, charts, maps, and other graphic aids found within nonfiction texts. Help your reader learn more about the different ways information can be displayed.

Table of Contents

Located at the front of the book, this list shows the big ideas within the text and the page numbers where they can be found.

Glossary

Located at the back of the book, the glossary defines key words and phrases that are related to the topic. These words and phrases can be found in the text in colored type.

Index

Located at the back of the book, an index is an alphabetical list of topics and the page numbers where they can be found.

With a little help and guidance about reading nonfiction, you can feel good about introducing a young reader to the world of *Little Mitchie* nonfiction books.

Mitchell Lane
PUBLISHERS

2001 SW 31st Avenue
Hallandale, FL 33009
www.mitchelllanepub.com

Little Mitchie

First Edition, 2025.

Author: Kim Thompson
Designer: Kathy Walsh
Editor: Luana Mitten

Names/credits: Kim Thompson
Title: All-Time Funniest Jokes
About Holidays / Compiled by Kim Thompson
Description: Hallandale, FL:
Mitchell Lane Publishers, [2025]

Series: All-Time Funniest Jokes
Library bound ISBN: 979-8-89260-264-8
Paperback ISBN: 979-8-89260-423-9
eBook ISBN: 979-8-89260-271-6

Little Mitchie is an imprint of
Mitchell Lane Publishers

PHOTO CREDITS
Alamy: Elena Elenaphotos21, 4; Lou Linwei, 5; SARAWUT PADUNGKWAN, 5; Visuals Stock, 8; North Wind Picture Archives, 12; Shutterstock: Memo Angeles, cover, 14, 19; V_ctoria, cover, 1, 22-23; KanKhem, 4, 6, 8, 10, 14, 16, 20; Rigoni Barbara, 4; Yuri Turkov, 6; Master1305, 6; studiostoks, 6; Reginast777, 7; Heri Yusuf, 7; Lidiia, 7; WESTOCK PRODUCTIONS, 8; Photographielove, 9; Nataliya Druchkova, 9; Serenko Natalia, 10; Sharomka, 10; phive, 11; tsyhun, 11; Anastasia Samorodova, 12; Stephen Chung, 13; Hari_Aprianto, 13; GoodFocused, 14; Fokasu Art, 14; AGCuesta, 15; dOMENZOR, 15; Roman Samborskyi, 16; Tim Carillet, 16; Zlata Ushakova, 17; HitToon, 17; schwarzhana, 17; Teguh Mujiono, 18; Markgraphics, 18; bilha golan, 19; Pixel-Shot, 20; TQ-graphics, 20; Diane Diederich, 21; caneraydin, 21

CONTENTS

CHINESE NEW YEAR 4
VALENTINE'S DAY 6
HOLI 8
EASTER 10
THE FOURTH OF JULY 12
THE DAY OF THE DEAD 14
THANKSGIVING 16
HANUKKAH 18
CHRISTMAS 20
MORE LAUGHS 22
HOW TO TELL A JOKE 22
GLOSSARY 23
INDEX 23
FURTHER READING 24
ON THE INTERNET 24
ABOUT THE JOKESTER 24

CHINESE NEW YEAR

Q: WHY DO CHINESE NEW YEAR MEALS TAKE SO LONG?

A: BECAUSE THEY TEND TO DRAG-ON!

Q: WHEN IS CHINESE NEW YEAR JUST NEW YEAR?

A: WHEN YOU ARE IN CHINA!

VALENTINE'S DAY

Q: HOW DO SNAKES SHOW THEIR LOVE ON VALENTINE'S DAY?
A: WITH HUGS AND HISSES!
Q: WHERE DID A COUPLE OF HAMBURGERS GO ON VALENTINE'S DAY?
A: TO THE MEATBALL!

HOLI

Q: WHAT'S THE BEST THING TO HAVE ON HOLI?

A: A SPLASHING GOOD TIME!

Q: WHO CAN YOU INVITE TO A HOLI PARTY?

A: ALL YOUR HUE-MAN FRIENDS!

Q: WHAT DO YOU CALL HOLI WITH NO COLORS?

A: A WASHOUT!

Q: HOW DO COLORS FEEL ABOUT A HOLI CELEBRATION?

A: THEY ARE DYE-ING TO GO!

EASTER

Q: WHY ARE BUNNIES SLEEPY WHEN EASTER COMES IN APRIL?
A: BECAUSE THEY'VE JUST HAD A LONG MARCH!
Q: WHAT DID THE KIDS DO WHEN THEY FOUND OUT THEIR EASTER TREATS WERE HIDDEN?
A: THEY DEMANDED AN EGGS-PLANATION!

Q: WHAT DAY DO EGGS HATE THE MOST?

A: FRY-DAY!

Q: WHERE DOES CHRISTMAS COME BEFORE EASTER?

A: IN THE DICTIONARY!

THE FOURTH OF JULY

Q: WHAT WAS THE MOST POPULAR DANCE IN 1776?

A: THE INDEPEN-DANCE!

Q: WHO DOESN'T GET THE DAY OFF ON THE FOURTH OF JULY?

A: FIRE WORKS!

Q: WHAT'S THE DIFFERENCE BETWEEN GEORGE WASHINGTON AND A DUCK?
A: GEORGE WASHINGTON HAS HIS FACE ON A BILL AND A DUCK HAS A BILL ON ITS FACE!
Q: WHAT DO AN AMERICAN FLAG AND A SAD CANDY CANE HAVE IN COMMON?
A: THEY ARE BOTH RED, WHITE, AND BLUE!

THE DAY OF THE DEAD

Q: WHAT SWEET TREAT IS NEVER PUT ON THE *OFRENDA* ON TIME?
A: CHOCO-LATE!
Q: WHAT INSTRUMENT DO THE COOLEST SKELETONS PLAY?
A: THE SAX-O-BONE!

THANKSGIVING

Q: WHY SHOULD YOU NEVER TELL A SECRET ON THANKSGIVING?
A: BECAUSE THE POTATOES HAVE EYES, THE CORN HAS EARS, AND THE BEANS STALK!
Q: WHAT IS A TURKEY'S FAVORITE DESSERT?
A: APPLE GOBBLER!

HANUKKAH

Q: WHICH HAND SHOULD YOU USE TO LIGHT THE MENORAH?
A: NEITHER. YOU SHOULD LIGHT IT WITH A CANDLE!
Q: HOW MANY POTATOES DOES IT TAKE TO MAKE POTATO PANCAKES?
A: A LATKE!

Q: WHY DID THE DREIDEL HAVE TO GO TO THE DOCTOR?
A: IT KEPT GETTING DIZZY!
Q: WHAT'S THE DIFFERENCE BETWEEN HANUKKAH AND A DRAGON?
A: ONE LASTS EIGHT NIGHTS AND THE OTHER ATE KNIGHTS!

CHRISTMAS

Q: HOW DO REINDEER DECORATE FOR CHRISTMAS?
A: WITH HORN-AMENTS!
Q: WHAT KIND OF PHOTOS DO SANTA'S HELPERS TAKE?
A: ELF-IES!

Q: WHAT DO SNOWMEN CALL THEIR SONS AND DAUGHTERS?

A: THEIR CHILL-DREN!

Q: WHAT IS IT CALLED WHEN SANTA TAKES A BREAK?

A: A SANTA PAUSE!

MORE LAUGHS

What is a cow's favorite night of the year? *Moo Year's Eve!*

Why didn't the groundhog want to come out on Groundhog Day? *It was having a bad lair day!*

Why do people wear shamrocks on St. Patrick's Day? *Because regular rocks are too heavy!*

How do pirates celebrate April Fools' Day? *They walk the prank!*

What's a good motto for Earth Day? *Don't leaf the Earth a mess!*

How do you fix a damaged jack-o-lantern for Halloween? *You use a pumpkin patch!*

HOW TO TELL A JOKE

1. Relax. If you feel awkward, your audience will too.
2. Don't rush. Give your joke some space and trust that it's a good one!
3. Vary your tone. Your voice should not be flat or boring.
4. Pause right before the punchline. This will add some drama!
5. End right on the punchline. Don't keep talking or try to explain.
6. If you don't get a laugh, that's okay. Try another joke!

GLOSSARY

"I GET IT NOW!"

Chinese New Year (CHYE-neez noo yeer): a 15-day celebration in January and March when people feast, visit relatives, attend festivals, and give children gifts of money in red envelopes

dreidel (DRAY-duhl): a four-sided toy spun like a top during a game of chance played at Hanukkah celebrations

Holi (HOH-lee): a festival in March when people cover each other with bright colors by throwing colored powders and splashing colored water from buckets and squirt guns

hue (hyoo): a color or shade of a color

Mandarin (MAN-duh-ruhn): a language spoken by many people in China; a type of duck native to China

menorah (muh-NOR-uh): a special holder for nine candles that is used during Hanukkah celebrations

ofrenda (oh-FREND-uh): an altar that is built for the Day of the Dead and filled with items that honor ancestors

pan de muerto (pan duh MWAIR-toh): a sweet bread made and eaten to celebrate the Day of the Dead

INDEX

bunnies 10
colors 9
dragon(s) 4, 19
eggs 10, 11
firecrackers 4
flag 13
latke 18
reindeer 20
Santa 20, 21
skeleton(s) 14, 15
snowmen 21
turkey 16, 17

FURTHER READING

Cheeky Monkey. *Hilarious Jokes*, Puns, Riddles & Pranks: *A Tickle-Your-Funny-Bone Book for Silly Kids Who Love to LOL*. Atglen, PA: Better Day Books, 2024.

Katz, Alan. *The Funniest Joke Book Ever for Kids!* New York: Scholastic, 2024.

Riddleland. *The Jumbo Book of Funny Jokes for Kids*. Prospect Park, PA: BCBM Holdings, 2023.

ON THE INTERNET

Good Housekeeping: 125 Knock Knock Jokes for Kids and Adults Who Love to Laugh https://www.goodhousekeeping.com/life/parenting/g36198919/knock-knock-jokes-for-kids/ Silly jokes to fool your family members and friends!

Parents: 100 Jokes for Kids That Will Actually Make You Laugh https://www.parents.com/fun/entertainment/14-jokes-for-kids-that-will-actually-make-you-laugh/ A source for Dad jokes, one-liners, puns, and more.

Today: 150 Funny Jokes That Will Get the Family Laughing https://www.today.com/parents/family/jokes-for-kids-rcna49138hat/Find jokes about seasons, animals, and more.

ABOUT THE JOKESTER

Kim Thompson is a teacher, writer, and editor. Things that make her laugh out loud include going down waterslides while holding her feet in the air, trying to balance a grape on her nose, and the dopey expressions that turtles get on their faces. She lives with her husband and two funny cats in Columbus, Ohio.